C000277502

SAMUEL PEPYS
AND HIS CIRCLE

Richard Ollard

NPG

Published in Great Britain by National Portrait Gallery Publications,
National Portrait Gallery, St Martin's Place, London WC2H 0HE

ISBN 1 85514 281 3

A catalogue record for this book is available from the British Library

Publishing Manager: Jacky Colliss Harvey
Series Editor: Susie Foster
Project Editor: Celia Jones
Series Designer: Karen Stafford
Printed by Clifford Press Ltd, Coventry

Front cover
Samuel Pepys, 1633–1703
John Hayls, 1666 (detail)
Oil on canvas, 75.6 x 62.9cm
© National Portrait Gallery (211)

For a complete catalogue of current publications,
please write to the address above, or visit our website on
http://www.npg.org.uk/pubs.htm

Contents

Samuel Pepys, John Hayls, 1666

INTRODUCTION

❦

'Sir, when a man is tired of London, he is tired of life, for there is in London all that life can afford.' Dr Johnson's famous judgement might equally be applied to Pepys. The range of his interests, the diversity of his pleasures, the vigour of his activity in public and private business, the reflectiveness that led him to record and to evaluate this multiplicity of experience, the communicableness of his humanity, give him a universality comparable with Shakespeare's. In a sense Pepys's circle was nothing less than the world of his time. Nothing bored him. Nothing escaped him. Yet for all this universality, he was intensely, supremely, individual. We should know him at once if he came into the room. The portraits of him on pages 4, 7 and 8, one in the prime of life, the others in successful middle age, would in any case make identification easy.

He was born in 1633, the son of a tailor in a very moderate way of business, in Salisbury Court, just off Fleet Street. His mother was of even humbler origin: her relations were butchers, fishmongers and such. The Pepyses extended their connections over a far wider social spectrum. Some of them were tradesmen, like the diarist's father, but a lot of them were lawyers and some were even on the fringes of the landed gentry in East Anglia, where the family is first recorded. However, it was the fortunate marriage of Samuel's great-aunt Paulina into the rich and prominent Montagu family that dealt Pepys his card of entry into the great world of public affairs, where he was to make his name and fortune.

Edward Montagu, Paulina's son, was to be by far the most important member of Pepys's family, but he can hardly be said to belong to Pepys's family circle. Rather, his place is in the circle of Pepys's naval and political colleagues. The family circle, Pepys's father and mother, his unsatisfactory brother Tom, his hardly less unsatisfactory sister Paulina (generally abbreviated to Pall) have left no visual record. Neither have the friends and relations with whom the rising young official enjoyed convivial evenings of music and dancing. Only the bust of his young wife Elizabeth (1640–69) in St Olave's, Hart Street, commissioned by her bereaved husband, survives to remind us of the domesticity brought to life in the *Diary*.

5

ELIZABETH PEPYS, after a marble attributed to John Bushnell, 1672

The *Diary* is virtually our only source for Elizabeth Pepys. We see her through the kaleidoscope of her husband's rapidly changing moods, tender and bullying, affectionate and irritable, jealous of her attractiveness to other men and guilty at his own infidelities. Pepys's heroic candour exposes his own meanness, compared with her generosity and readiness to please him. He was very much the senior partner – she was only fifteen when he married her and he was in his early twenties. Her family were impoverished Huguenot refugees though Elizabeth had had what little education she had managed to acquire at a convent in Paris – another dangerous disrecommendation in the fanatically anti-Catholic England of the seventeenth century. The imprudence of the marriage is evidence of its passion, reinforced by the stormy passages so vividly recorded in the *Diary*. Although Elizabeth was not a member of his circle as an equal in it, Pepys did encourage her to share his musical and artistic tastes and admired the promise she showed in singing and painting. Her early death, only a few months after the *Diary* closes in 1669 ended his most intimate relationship.

Of Pepys's boyhood we have virtually no record. A boy of nine when the Civil War broke out in 1642, it seems probable that he was sent to the grammar school in Huntingdon, where his uncle had property nearby. At the end of the war he went to St Paul's and we know that he was still at school there when he witnessed the execution of Charles I in January 1649. Equipped with a leaving exhibition he went up to Magdalene College, Cambridge, taking his degree in 1654. In that year or the next he became some kind of a servant, not a secretary exactly nor yet a steward but something of that order, to his eminent cousin, eking out this modest position by taking service as a clerk to George Downing (after whom Downing Street is named), then an official of the Exchequer.

SAMUEL PEPYS
John Closterman,
*c.*1690–1700

SAMUEL PEPYS, Sir Godfrey Kneller, n.d.

When Montagu was charged with taking the fleet over to Holland to bring back Charles II in the spring of 1660 he offered Pepys the post of secretary. From then on Pepys's career was made. Clerk of the Acts, Secretary to the Admiralty, Treasurer of the Tangier Committee, Surveyor-General of the Victualling of the Royal Navy, Clerk of the Privy Seal, the Government jobs came in pell-mell. And each one offered, besides a salary, an almost unlimited opportunity for feathering one's nest. For the rest of his life Pepys was to be comfortably off and latterly very rich.

This enabled him to indulge his pleasures and to cultivate his tastes, even to become a patron: 'a very great cherisher of learned men of whom he had the conversation' as his friend for forty years, John Evelyn, wrote of him on his death in 1703. His superb library, preserved in its entirety at Magdalene College, Cambridge, shows the depth and breadth of his intellectual and literary interests. The *Diary* is eloquent of his passion for the theatre and, above all, for music 'the thing of the world that I love most'. His eye for painting was keen and he knew most of the leading artists of his day. The division between the sciences and the arts, 'the two cultures' in C.P. Snow's famous phrase, had not yet appeared. Pepys was an early Fellow and ultimately President, of the new-born Royal Society. At the height of the Dutch War, he, the right-hand of the Navy as George Monck called him, took the day off to be rowed upriver while reading a treatise on the hydrostatics. His professional life, too, nourished his intellectual curiosity. Not only ships and shipbuilding but the wider implications of seapower led him to amass materials for a 'History of the Marine' which would have taken in, besides ordinary naval history, exploration and discovery, colonisation and seaborne trade.

The *Diary*, to which allusion has already been made, is one of the great texts of English literature, of English history, almost one might say of English civilisation. It is certainly the reason why we have all heard of Pepys. Since it was first published, a century and a half after it had been written, it has never been out of print.

It covers a mere nine years – from January 1660 to May 1669. But what years! The death-throes of the English Republic, the Restoration of the Monarchy in May 1660, the Plague of 1665, the Fire of London in 1666, the great battles of the Second Dutch War, as hard-fought as any in the history of the Royal Navy, the humiliation with which it ended when the Dutch broke into the main fleet base in the Medway and towed away the flagship (her stern can still be seen in the Rijksmuseum at Amsterdam). Through all this period Pepys was uniquely well-placed to observe, and he was one of the most observant men who ever lived. The freedom with which he expressed his opinions of great persons from the King downwards made this a highly dangerous document. He always kept it under lock and key and it was written in short-hand, which accounts for its lying unread in his library for more than a century after his death.

Pepys discontinued the *Diary* because eye-trouble convinced him that he was going blind. In fact this cleared up with the help of spectacles. He was to live for another thirty-four years and to become one of the most creative public servants in our history.

Politics and economics – a word only recently coined and hardly in circulation even among educated men – were his constant preoccupation and led him to a range of important friendships and acquaintances. And then there were his day-to-day colleagues at the Navy Board, some of them highly efficient like Sir William Coventry or Sir George Carteret, some of them amiable muddlers like Sir John Mennes. Most important of all there were the Sea Officers as Pepys and his contemporaries called them, Naval officers as we should say: Montagu himself, Monck, Prince Rupert, the Duke of York, Sir Robert Holmes, Sir Christopher Myngs, Sir John Harman, Sir John Narborough and many others. It was an age rich in achievement in every sphere, and in many of them Pepys was either personally engaged or an alert and informed spectator.

SUGGESTIONS FOR FURTHER READING

Far the most comprehensive single source of information about every aspect of Pepys's world is the Companion Volume (vol.10, Bell & Hyman, London, 1983) to the great edition of the *Diary* by Robert Latham and William Matthews. It is, however, designed for reference, not for continuous reading.

The text of the *Diary* itself in the preceding nine volumes (1970–76) is, of course, incomparable – and the annotation of the Latham and Matthews edition delightfully removes every difficulty.

Of biographies, Sir Arthur Bryant's three volumes, *Pepys: The Man in the Making* (1933), *The Years of Peril* (1935) and *The Saviour of the Navy* (1938), published by Cambridge University Press, have, for all their copiousness and colour, the disadvantage of incompleteness. The third volume ends with Pepys's fall from office in 1688. The present writer's *Pepys: A Biography* (Hodder & Stoughton, London, 1974, several times reissued under different imprints) contains two chapters directly bearing on the friendships and interests of his long retirement.

For a general survey of the period, David Ogg's *England in the Reign of Charles II* (Clarendon Press, Oxford, 1934; reprinted 1966) offers a panorama appropriate to Pepys's many-sidedness.

NAVAL COLLEAGUES: ADMINISTRATORS, TARPAULINS AND GENTLEMEN

EDWARD MONTAGU, 1ST EARL OF SANDWICH, after Sir Peter Lely, c.1660

Edward Montagu, 1st Earl of Sandwich (1625–72)

❦

Edward Montagu was one of the star performers in the age of civil war and rapid political change that followed the virtual collapse of Charles I's government in 1641. Raising a regiment for Parliament as a young man of nineteen, he so much impressed Cromwell that he was given a colonelcy in the New Model Army. Under the Protectorate he was made a member of the Council of State and in 1656 joined with the great admiral Blake in command of the fleet. Robert Blake (1599–1657) was far the greatest admiral that England had yet produced. Alike for his success as a fighting leader, for his grasp of maritime strategy and for the devotion he inspired in his seamen, he is the only possible rival to Nelson. Nelson indeed, never given to false modesty, famously recognised this: 'I do not count myself equal to Blake.' That Blake is so little known to the generality of his countrymen is explained by the fact of his service having been exclusive to the Republic that had been formed on the execution of Charles I. Even as late as 1912 King George V refused to allow a Dreadnought to be named after him.

In 1659, after the death of Oliver and the fall of Richard Cromwell, Montagu commanded the fleet and Monck the army that brought about the immensely popular restoration of Charles II. Monck was made a duke, Montagu an earl, and both were in a position to promote their own friends and relations. It was thus that Pepys became in 1660 Clerk of the Acts, in effect Secretary, to the Navy Board. This is what he meant when he remarked a few years later 'Chance, not merit, brought me into the navy'.

Montagu's absences at sea had opened his eyes to his young cousin's talents as a political observer and reporter. A Commander-in-Chief abroad needed to know what were the pressures on the Government at home and what it was thinking of doing next. Pepys's curiosity, his love of gossip, his eager sociability, combined to make him a marvellous source, as every reader of the *Diary* can see.

Montagu's claims to the supreme command in the Second Dutch War (1665–7) were strong: but room had to be found for the King's brother, James, Duke of York, as Lord High Admiral and for his cousin Prince

EDWARD MONTAGU, 1ST EARL OF SANDWICH
Sir Peter Lely, *c.*1655–9

Rupert. Even so, Montagu distinguished himself in the opening action, the battle off Lowestoft, and was subsequently entrusted with the command of the squadron detailed to intercept De Ruyter, convoying homeward-bound merchantmen from the Dutch East Indies. De Ruyter slipped through, but some rich prizes were taken. Montagu's carelessness in not enforcing the strict regulations to prevent looting was seized on by his enemies. To protect him, Charles II and Clarendon appointed him ambassador to Madrid, where he was a conspicuous success.

Pepys's failure to keep in touch with him during these years of absence led to a coolness between them. On the outbreak of the Third Dutch War in 1672 Montagu was once again appointed a flag officer under the Duke of York and once again was in the hottest of the initial action off the Suffolk coast, in which he lost his life. He was given a State Funeral in Westminster Abbey, a fitting recognition of his outstanding services.

14

Sir William Coventry (1627–86)

❧

Professionalism was the first principle of Pepys's life. More than any other figure in our history he was responsible for professionalising the Royal Navy, that is, making it into a wholetime, permanent force with a career structure. Even in the arts – painting, the theatre, music – in which he was necessarily a dilettante, he expected professionalism in the practitioners whom he admired or patronised. His own career was founded on professionalism. Chance, not merit, may have brought him into the Navy but from the moment he arrived at the Navy Office in Seething Lane, hard by the Tower, he made administrative efficiency and the acquiring of professional knowledge in every department of the Board's responsibilities his first and transcendent objectives.

In this context, Sir William Coventry was the colleague whom Pepys most admired. To a great extent Pepys tried to model himself on him but could not achieve Coventry's high-minded determination not to accept bribes, a principle that Coventry even tried to introduce into government service in exchange for an increase in salaries. Pepys, with his instinct for efficiency, saw the merit of this proposal but was not surprised that it did not find favour. Charles II was hardly the man to clean up the business of government. Coventry, indeed, was a bolder man than his young admirer, as his circumstances enabled him to be. The son of a much respected Lord Keeper under Charles I, his social and financial position left him free to be his own man. As a very young man he had fought for the King and followed Charles II into exile, but, finding no opening for his talents, returned to live quietly under Cromwell. At the Restoration, James, Duke of York, made him his private secretary as well as his secretary in his capacity as Lord High Admiral. This brought him a place, though not an office, on the Navy Board.

Coventry had been elected to Parliament in 1661, the so-called Long Parliament of the Restoration (it was not dissolved till 1679) where he rapidly made a name as one of the best, perhaps the best, debaters. His fearless integrity did not endear him to the King or to the Duke of York, who liked their politicians pliant. On the other hand his outstanding ability (admitted even by Clarendon, the King's chief minister, who had always disliked him) and his standing in the House of Commons made him a valuable servant. The split came in 1667, when Coventry led the

SIR WILLIAM COVENTRY, John Riley, n.d.

Parliamentary attack on Clarendon whom everyone (except the Duke of York who had married his daughter) was glad to make the scapegoat for the misconduct of the Dutch War, culminating in the shame of the Medway disaster. James dismissed his secretary for what he regarded as personal disloyalty and the King, who had always resented Coventry's dispassionate intelligence, seized the first opportunity of getting rid of him altogether. There was no public servant whom Pepys held in such unqualified esteem: 'the ability and integrity of Sir William Coventry in all the King's concernments I do and must admire.' Coventry himself shewed his usual penetration when he told Pepys, at the very moment of his apparent success in the dismissal of Clarendon, 'that the serving a Prince that minds not his business is most unhappy for them that serve him well, and an unhappiness so great that he will never have more to do with a war, under him'.

Sir John Harman (1625–73)

The sea officers with whom Pepys's life was bound up were at the time, and have been generally since, classified under two categories: the Tarpaulins and the Gentlemen. The tarpaulins, as their nickname suggests, were what Pepys called 'bred seamen', that is they had followed the sea as a means of livelihood, in merchant ships or on whaling voyages or less ambitious fishery. Under the aggressive, expansionist foreign policy of Cromwell the State Navy had grown to a formidable size, offering more or less continuous employment with attractive prospects of wealth and public honour. Most, indeed practically all, the tarpaulins were thus by definition men who had served under the Commonwealth and Protectorate governments, of whom a good example is Sir John Harman. Harman first appears as Captain of a forty-gun ship in the First Dutch War (1652–4), subsequently serving under Blake in the Mediterranean and at the great victory of Santa Cruz in the Canaries, when the entire Spanish plate fleet was sunk while riding at anchor. In the Second and Third Dutch Wars (1665–7 and 1672–4) he was in the thick of the bloodiest actions: in both he was severely wounded and in both he distinguished himself as a flag officer, winning a brilliant victory in the West Indies.

Sir John Harman, Admiral of the Blue, 1673

Sᴏɪʀ Jᴏʜɴ Hᴀʀᴍᴀɴ, studio of Sir Peter Lely, *c.*1666

Sir John Mennes (1599–1671) and William, 2nd Viscount Brouncker (1620?–84)

William, 2nd Viscount Brouncker
Possibly after Sir Peter Lely, *c.*1674

Pepys's professionalism and administrative zeal frequently brought him into collision with his colleagues; older, much more experienced men, such as Sir William Penn and Sir William Batten, both of whom had held high command at sea in the Civil War on the Parliament side, and Sir John Mennes, a Royalist whose career as a sea officer reached back to the reign of James I. Pepys enjoyed his company over a convivial glass: Mennes was an amusing conversationalist and a ready composer of ribald

SIR JOHN MENNES, unknown artist, ?1640

verse, but as an administrator it is impossible to better Sir William Coventry's inspired image: 'like a lapwing; that all he did was to keep a flutter to keep others from the nest that they would find.'

Penn and Batten were tarpaulins of the tarpaulins. They had followed the sea from boyhood, and their familiarity with every detail of seamanship and ship construction meant that Pepys had to address himself to mastering all these technicalities if he were to be able to hold his own at the Navy Board. Mennes was a gentleman officer *par excellence*. It is appropriate that he was the officer entrusted by Charles I with bringing Rubens over to England.

Of his other colleagues in naval administration, one of the most prominent was William, Viscount Brouncker, the first President of the Royal Society. Like Pepys he had no antecedent experience of naval affairs, but a peer who was distinguished in the circle of experimental philosophers might be expected to have something to contribute to the deliberations of the Navy Board. Besides their common interest in science, Brouncker shared Pepys's love and knowledge of music. The curious mixture of insouciant irresponsibility with the formidable skills of Charles II's navy is exemplified by Brouncker's younger brother Henry, a courtier in the suite of the Duke of York. After the great victory off Lowestoft in 1665 when the Dutch, in disorderly flight, were at the mercy of the English, Henry Brouncker, pretending to have the Duke's authority, ordered sail to be shortened, thus allowing the enemy to escape.

Sir Robert Holmes (1622–92) and Sir Frescheville Holles (1642–72)

Two gentlemen officers with whom Pepys had somewhat stormy relations were Sir Robert Holmes and Sir Frescheville Holles, arrestingly portrayed in one of Lely's finest double-portraits. A gentleman officer was equally by definition Royalist, not Cromwellian still less Parliamentarian, in political sympathy. Some of them, like Frescheville Holles, were too young to have served in the Civil War but Holmes, as a junior cavalry officer, had won the good opinion of Prince Rupert and had followed him into exile in 1646. When in 1648 a great part of the Parliamentary fleet mutinied and went over to Holland to put itself under the command of the Prince of Wales, the future Charles II, Rupert was appointed to command the ships that did not return to England and their original obedience. Holmes joined him and served under him in precarious buccaneering voyages without any proper base. First of all to southern Ireland, then Lisbon, then to the Mediterranean, where Blake caught up with them and destroyed all but a couple of ships, then down the Atlantic coast of Africa, across by the Cape Verde islands to the West Indies and back, at last, to the mouth of the Loire in 1652, it was an apprenticeship to seafaring as arduous as that of most tarpaulins and certainly as adventurous. Holmes was at once employed by the restored Monarchy. Experienced sea officers of such impeccable Royalist antecedents were in short supply. He was sent in command of two expeditions down the Atlantic coast of Africa in 1661 and in 1663 in support of the Royal African Company against the much better-established Dutch. On the second voyage he interpreted his instructions in so aggressive a spirit, capturing Dutch forts and making prize of their vessels, as to make a war more or less inevitable. In the course of it Holmes, as Rear-Admiral of the Red, carried out one of the most successful raids against the merchant shipping on which Dutch power was based. Known as 'Holmes's Bonfire', well over a hundred ships went up in smoke in the anchorage of the Vlie, a natural harbour sheltered by the islands of Vlie and Schelling on the coast of Friesland.

But before that Holmes and Pepys had had words at a meeting of the Navy Board in 1663 that might easily, as Pepys apprehensively recorded

in the *Diary*, have led to a duel. To Pepys's relief Holmes relented. They were brought into contact again in the Third Dutch War, and, at the very end of Pepys's career, when William III's invasion fleet was in the Channel, both men were unfaltering in their loyalty to James II. In 1690

Pepys even sought Holmes's help in his unavailing attempts to regain a seat in Parliament.

The last of the sea officers here illustrated is Sir Frescheville Holles, Holmes's partner in the double-portrait. He is painted in half-profile, brandishing his sword, perhaps because he had lost his other arm in the Battle of the Four Days (1–4 June 1666). Holles was a courtier-captain who also held a commission in the Guards and sat in Parliament, where as a partisan of the Duke of Buckingham, he was apt to be a vigorous critic of the Navy Board. He was exactly the sort of officer that Pepys was fondest of inveighing against, undisciplined, hard-drinking, hard-swearing, in a word unprofessional. But his record as a fighting leader was impressive enough for Holmes to choose to be commemorated with him and to commend his service in the opening battle of the Third Dutch War. Two months later he was killed at the Battle of Sole Bay (May 1672).

PETER PETT (1610–70)

Professionalism, it has been remarked, was the key to Pepys's own approval, even perhaps where he thought such obvious virtues as courage and honesty were wanting. Such was the case with the famous shipwright, Peter Pett. He was the son of an equally famous shipbuilder Phineas Pett, and the Pett clan, whose ramifications would baffle all but the most seasoned genealogist, occupied practically all the important positions in the yards along the Thames and the Medway, and had done so well before Pepys came on the scene. In this picture he stands in front of the great and beautiful ship, the *Sovereign of the Seas*, the pride of Charles I's navy, herself asserting in her name the high claims of the Stuart monarchy. Pepys evidently did not like him and with the rest of his colleagues on the Navy Board was relieved and delighted to have him made another scapegoat for the Medway disaster of 1667, for which they might more justly have been called to account.

> *All our miscarriages on Pett must fall:*
> *His name alone seems fit to answer all.*
> *Whose counsel first did this mad War beget?*
> *Who all commands sold through the Navy?* Pett.
> *Who all our ships exposed in Chatham's Net?*
> *Who should it be but the* Phanatick Pett?
> Pett, *the Sea Architect, in making Ships,*
> *Was the first cause of all these Naval slips:*
> *Had he not built, none of these faults had bin;*
> *If no Creation, there had been no Sin.*

The wit and force of Marvell's satire have assured him his place in history.

PETER PETT, possibly after Sir Peter Lely, ?18th century

THE KING, THE COURT AND POLITICS

CHARLES II (1630–85)

Only five years after the Medway disaster, England was again at war with the Dutch and Pepys was again, in administrative terms, the right-hand of the Navy. By this time Sir William Coventry had become the most formidable critic of the King's pro-French policy of the 1670s, and, while Pepys could not afford to support Coventry's opinions in too public a manner, he complained in his Naval Minutes, those private reflections he jotted down mostly in his retirement, of the King's frivolity and, as it seemed to him, sheer irresponsibility.

CHARLES II, studio of John Riley, *c*.1680–85

CHARLES II, studio of John Michael Wright, c.1660–65

However, Pepys was impressed by the King's mastery of naval detail and his intellectual apprehension of what it all amounted to (which is what is signified by the, to us, odd use of the word 'mathematic'). He joined him with his brother James, Duke of York, and Pepys's own patron the Earl of Sandwich in a famous judgement: 'The King, Duke and he [Sandwich] the most mathematick Admirals England ever had.' The King, in fact never commanded a fleet at sea as the other two did, so that the interpretation given above seems inescapable.

Pepys was not the only man to observe this combination of capacity and disinclination to use it. It is the keynote of the prose portrait *The Character of King Charles II* drawn by one of his ablest ministers, the Marquess of Halifax. Pepys became one of the most highly placed, and highly paid, servants of the King, but he was never a courtier, still less an intimate. Their relationship was always easy. The King was a shrewd judge of men and knew Pepys's value. He sometimes shewed his appreciation but perhaps the nearest approach to intimacy was when in October 1680 he dictated to him his account of his adventures when he was on the run after the Battle of Worcester in 1651.

The King's love of pleasure evoked conflicting reactions in Pepys. On the one hand he envied him the embraces of Lady Castlemaine: on the other he disapproved of the neglect of business to which his love of pleasure contributed.

That the King recognised the value of his most expert servant in the most important, and most expensive, of all departments of state is clear from many instances, culminating in the unprecedented appointment, at the very end of Charles II's reign, to the Secretaryship of the Admiralty. It is this professional relation that gives Pepys's portrayal of Charles II its special quality. The King's laziness, his unreliability, his frivolity, are tellingly stated: but his acuteness, his understanding of naval affairs, his coolness in times of danger, are never underplayed.

JAMES II (1633–1701)

JAMES II, Sir Peter Lely, *c.*1665–70

W ith Charles II's brother and successor, James, Duke of York, Pepys had a great deal to do. Straightforward to a fault (dissimulation is, as Halifax pointed out in the character of Charles 'a Jewel of the Crown'),

JAMES II
Unknown artist,
late 17th century

brave, and loyal to the men who served him, he was in most ways the antithesis of his brother. James had real military talent: as a young man in exile he had won golden opinions and rapid promotion in the French army. As an admiral his coolness in action was universally admired and, for so naturally obstinate a man, he shewed a wise readiness to learn from the experts who sailed with him just as he did with his brilliant administrators, Coventry and Pepys. Pepys's own loyalty to him was complete. After the Revolution of 1688 he refused to take the oaths to William and Mary, thus exposing himself to the penalty of double taxation as well as ending his official career.

Few English kings have been so totally devoid of political antennae. In spite of ample warning the Revolution of 1688 came on James II like a thunderclap. The disloyalty of men he had trusted unmanned him. His reactions, inept and indecisive, made the transition to William and Mary easier than anyone could have hoped. He retired to France, making, with French support, an unsuccessful attempt to recover his throne by raising his Irish Catholic subjects against his usurping son-in-law. The Siege of Londonderry and the Battle of the Boyne have left their mark on Anglo-Irish relations.

PRINCE RUPERT (1619–82)

With Holmes's patron, Prince Rupert (Charles I's nephew, son of his sister Elizabeth, the Winter Queen, and Frederick, Elector Palatine), Pepys's relations were never happy. In the *Diary* he is dismissed as empty and arrogant: 'Prince Robert [Rupert] doth nothing but swear and laugh a little, with an oath or two, and that's all he doth.' This is Rupert as a fellow member of the Tangier Committee, whose Treasurership Pepys counted 'one of the best flowers in my garden'. As a Commander-in-Chief in the Second and Third Dutch Wars there was real antagonism; Pepys accusing him of, or implying his responsibility for, mishandling of scarce naval stores while Rupert roundly attacked Pepys for failure to maintain essential supplies.

PRINCE RUPERT, COUNT PALATINE
Studio of Sir Peter Lely, *c.*1670

Rupert's versatility has been overshadowed by his well-established reputation as the dashing cavalry commander of the Civil War. Dash and daring were by no means his only military qualities. On two crucial occasions his professional advice, against besieging Gloucester in 1643 and against seeking battle at Naseby in 1645, was overridden with disastrous results. His talents as a seaman have been neglected, as have his scientific experiments in surgery conducted on himself and in the development of the mezzotint. Born and brought up abroad, never really at home in English society or in the court of Charles II, he remains, aloof, distinguished, solitary.

GEORGE MONCK, 1ST DUKE OF ALBEMARLE, studio of Sir Peter Lely, 1665–6

George Monck,
1st Duke of Albemarle (1608–70)

In the campaign of 1666 Rupert was Joint Commander-in-Chief with George Monck, 1st Duke of Albemarle. Both men ought to have won Pepys's whole-hearted approval, since both were professionals first and last, and Rupert in addition was accomplished both as a scientist and an artist. Both had spent their lives in the profession of arms by land and sea: both had put themselves to school in foreign armies, Rupert with the Habsburg Emperor and Monck with the Dutch. Monck, as we have seen, was generous in his recognition of Pepys's services, but the compliment was not returned. Monck is repeatedly described as a 'blockhead' though his courage and his patriotism are grudgingly conceded. Part of the reason for this may unquestionably be found in the fierce rivalry between Monck and Pepys's patron, Montagu, the two men who had between them brought about the Restoration and were thereafter often at odds over the division of the spoils.

Monck, born into a Devon family of some standing, as a younger son had had to make his own way in the world. To have been raised from the status of a commoner to that of a duke in one stroke, as he was at the Restoration, was a remarkable achievement. While a prisoner of war in the Tower (he had been captured in 1644 as a Royalist officer) he married his washerwoman, who seems to have added ill nature and bad manners to her other disadvantages.

ANTHONY ASHLEY COOPER, 1ST EARL OF SHAFTESBURY (1621–83)

Of all the politicians with whom Pepys had to do (apart from his cousin and Sir William Coventry, who were his close associates) the ablest and most active was Anthony Ashley Cooper, created Baron Ashley in 1661 and Earl of Shaftesbury in 1672. Pepys came across him directly as a colleague on the Tangier Committee and indirectly as Chancellor of the Exchequer from 1661–72 and Lord Chancellor from 1672–3. Shaftesbury, as he is known to history, had changed sides during the Civil War and early established himself as an opponent to the absolutist tendencies of the restored monarchy, particularly as manifested in the heir presumptive, James, Duke of York. In the later years of the reign Shaftesbury came out as the founder of the Whig party, determined to exclude James from the succession on the grounds of his Roman Catholicism.

The campaign over the Exclusion Bill reminded the nation of the tension that had preceded the Civil War: 'Forty-one is come again'. It reached its crisis at the Parliament of Oxford in 1681, when Shaftesbury and his allies actually appeared in arms. But the King had laid his plans more skilfully than his father and dissolved the Parliament before Shaftesbury could secure his objective – before, indeed, there was any opportunity for motion or debate. Shaftesbury fled the country and the Whigs were in total disarray until James II's undisguised attempt to force a wildly unpopular policy on the country brought about the Revolution of 1688. As a servant of the monarchy and particularly of James, Pepys found himself on the opposite side to Shaftesbury but he clearly recognised his formidable intelligence.

ANTHONY ASHLEY COOPER, 1ST EARL OF SHAFTESBURY, after John Greenhill, c.1672–3

EDWARD HYDE,
1ST EARL OF CLARENDON (1609–74)

The other political Titan, an ageing Titan, whom Pepys found much more congenial was Edward Hyde, 1st Earl of Clarendon.

> *And endeed, I am mad in love with my Lord Chancellor, for he doth comprehend and speak as well, and with the greatest easiness and authority, that ever I saw in my life. I did never observe how much easier a man doth speak, when he knows all the company to be below him, than in him; for though he spoke endeed excellent well, yet his manner and freedom of doing it, as if he played with and was informing only all the rest of the company, was mighty pretty.*

This is Clarendon at a meeting of the Tangier Committee in 1666, old, arthritic, gouty, out of touch and out of sympathy with the frivolous, dissolute, indecent company preferred by Charles II. The portrait of him here reproduced shows him in the vigour of his prime, one of the wisest, most cultivated, and most articulate of all English statesmen.

Clarendon's misfortune was that he and his friends who did all they could to prevent the Civil War and, once it had started, to end it by negotiation not by military triumph, were never able to get Charles I to back them. Perhaps – who can guess the ebb and flow of that Protean mind? – left to himself, the King would have been ready to do so. But he never was left to himself and, in the opinion of many who knew him, was too distrustful of his own judgement. In any case when he saw that he was likely to be defeated and might be made prisoner he was clear and emphatic in choosing Hyde as the counsellor and guide for his heir, a choice that was amply vindicated by the Restoration. Clarendon came into power as an old man who had been out of the country for fourteen years. Pepys, for all his unstinted admiration, saw clearly that in the world of intrigue and day-to-day political management, Clarendon was no match for his enemies and rivals. 'My Lord Chancellor is upon his back, past ever getting up again.' Clarendon's fall in 1667, precipitated by the Medway disaster for which, like Pett, he was a convenient scapegoat, opened the way for him in a second efflorescence to produce a literary

EDWARD HYDE, 1ST EARL OF CLARENDON, after Adriaen Hanneman, *c.*1648–55

masterpiece, *The History of the Rebellion and Civil Wars in England*, worthy of the circle of his young manhood, the circle of Selden and Ben Jonson, of Falkland and Chillingworth. The first volume, published a generation after his death, came out in time for Pepys to read it and to write an ecstatic letter of praise to his son.

Η δὲ μετάνοια αὐτὴ φιλοσοφίας ἀρχὴ γίνεται.

JOHN EVELYN, Robert Walker, 1648

SOCIAL LIFE AND
INTELLECTUAL PLEASURES

JOHN EVELYN (1620–1706)

❧

John Evelyn was one of the two men (Sir William Coventry is the other) on whom Pepys consciously tried to model himself. In the group portrait, illustrated on page 44, Evelyn, in late middle age, is holding a copy of his famous book on trees, *Silva*. The book symbolises two important sides of Evelyn's nature, the connoisseur *par excellence*, the *arbiter elegantiae* – how inevitable the terms of fashionable European taste – in gardening, sculpture, engraving, and, on the other side, the scientific dendrologist who saw the necessity of a policy for tree planting to the maintenance of a navy composed of wooden ships.

From the first Pepys and Evelyn were brought together by this consonance of intellectual and aesthetic interests and the conduct of naval affairs. Evelyn had married into a naval family. He had a fine house at Deptford near the navy yard – rented by Peter the Great on his visit to England with his entourage, succinctly described by Evelyn's steward 'a houseful of Russians, and right nasty'. In the Dutch Wars he served as Commissioner for the Sick and Hurt and Pepys would have liked to have him as a colleague on the Navy Board. Both men were early and prominent Fellows of the Royal Society and Evelyn's range was, as Pepys would have been the first to admit, far wider and more searching than his own. He was among the earliest champions of the extraordinary gifts of Sir Christopher Wren and

SIR CHRISTOPHER WREN
Sir Godfrey Kneller, 1711

41

the discoverer of Grinling Gibbons. His collection of prints was the model and inspiration of Pepys's.

Pious, refined, delicate – almost, looking at the portrait of him as a young man, one had said exquisite – he did not share Pepys's avid sexual appetite nor, it must be admitted, his vivacity. Evelyn's *Diary* reads more like a work of reference than a record of a stream of consciousness. Some parts of it describing his European travels are indeed copied straight from guidebooks. But when he does sketch a character, for instance Charles II or Arlington, he is not stiff or priggish. The friendship, the real, deep, affectionate friendship, of the two men is one of the great charms of Pepys's circle.

WILL HEWER (1642–1715),
SIR JAMES HOUBLON (1629?–1700),
SIR ANTHONY DEANE (1638?–1721)
AND THOMAS GALE (1635?–1702)

❦

The group portrait illustrated here represents the circle of Pepys's old age and retirement, yet it preserves the range and diversity of his taste and curiosity and reaches back in some of its members to the days of his early active life at the Navy Board. The portrait of Evelyn, at the top, is surpassed in human warmth only by that of Pepys's loyalest and ablest assistant, Will Hewer, portrayed here in the bottom right-hand corner. Hewer originally joined Pepys as part-servant, part-office clerk, but rapidly rose to assist and eventually to succeed Pepys in some of his appointments. His uncle had been a leading naval official under the Protectorate, moving at the Restoration to the even more lucrative East India Company. It was from this source that Hewer drew his enormous wealth, enabling him to buy houses to the south of the Strand and a mansion out at Clapham in which Pepys spent his declining years. When the Revolution of 1688 spelled the end of Pepys's career Hewer wrote him a letter which his old master endorsed 'a letter of great tendernesse at a time of difficulty':

> *I know you will chearefully acquiesce in what ever circumstance God-Almighty shall think most propper for you, which I hope may prove more to your satisfaction than you can imagine; you may rest assured that I am wholly yours, and that you shall never want the utmost of my constant, faithfull and personall service.*

The same loyalty had been shewn at an earlier crisis by Sir James Houblon, who is here portrayed immediately above Hewer. The Houblons were a Huguenot émigré family with an astonishing breadth of trading connections and a financial expertise that provided the foundation for the Bank of England. Sir James, one of Pepys's most trusted friends, had risked unpopularity by visiting him in the Tower at the height of the Popish Plot, a ruthless and formidable attempt to frame

SAMUEL PEPYS (CENTRE), WITH (CLOCKWISE) JOHN EVELYN, SIR JAMES HOUBLON, WILL HEWER, THOMAS GALE AND SIR ANTHONY DEANE, n.d.

prominent supporters of the Duke of York as engaged in a treasonable conspiracy. As its name suggests it was designed to appeal to the fear and hatred of aggressive, militant Catholicism which seemed to seventeenth-century Englishmen to be carrying all before it everywhere in Europe. The cultivated mercantile Huguenot society, at home in European, not merely English, ways of life and thought, was highly congenial to Pepys.

Of the remaining two intimates on this most intimate page, Sir Anthony Deane and Dr Thomas Gale, Deane had shared the dangers of the Popish Plot. Indeed, he had shared almost the whole of Pepys's professional and political career – both had sat in Parliament for the Admiralty borough of Harwich under Charles II and James II. Deane was, above all, an outstanding professional. Among all the distinguished English shipwrights of the late seventeenth century Deane stood out, not only for the success of his designs and for the demand he was in (Louis XIV was among his clients) but also for the artistic elegance of his drawings, some of which Pepys collected for his library. Deane was already employed at Woolwich when Pepys was appointed Clerk of the Acts and they remained colleagues for thirty years and friends for life. But it was very much a professional friendship. Although Deane was elected Fellow of the Royal Society and served on its Council he does not appear to have had the discursive curiosity so characteristic of its early members.

Thomas Gale was, on the other hand, a more typical Fellow in the variety of his learning. A scholar of Westminster under Dr Busby (who was as famous for flogging his unfortunate pupils as Dr Keate at Eton a century later), he became Regius Professor of Greek at Cambridge and then High Master of St Paul's before ending his days as Dean of York. Besides his productive and wide-ranging classical scholarship he was also, like Humphrey Wanley, a notable collector of manuscripts and corresponded with Pepys, whose cousin he had married, in this common interest. His son Roger was as good an antiquary as his father and was one of the young scholars in whom the ageing Pepys took a benevolent interest.

HUMPHREY WANLEY (1672–1726)
AND RICHARD BENTLEY (1662–1742)

Sir Frescheville Holles, the gentleman officer portrayed by Lely (page 24) was the son of a very different sort of man, the antiquary Gervase Holles, whose great collection of manuscript material towards a 'History of Lincolnshire' had been largely destroyed when his house was plundered by Parliamentary troops during the Civil War. Pepys had a number of friends who, like the elder Holles, were active in searching out and preserving manuscripts of historical or literary importance. Among the learned men Pepys cherished, in John Evelyn's phrase, were two of the

HUMPHREY WANLEY, Thomas Hill, 1717

greatest in our history, Humphrey Wanley, the palaeographer to whose labours the Bodleian and the British Library owe so many of their treasures, and Richard Bentley, the classical scholar who was, after Pepys's death, to rule over Trinity College, Cambridge, with a rod of iron. Both, as can be seen from their dates, were young men when Pepys's official career had come to an end and he had leisure and resources to devote to the branches of learning that had always interested him.

RICHARD BENTLEY, after Sir James Thornhill, 1710

DR JOHN WALLIS (1616–1703)

Cambridge was Pepys's own university (he had even toyed with the suggestion that he should offer himself as a candidate for the Provostship of King's when it fell vacant in 1681), but it was on Oxford that the scholarly interests of his last years centred. The Bodleian was then by far the greatest library in England and it was there that the splendid portrait of Dr Wallis, which Pepys commissioned from Kneller as a present to the University, was to hang for a couple of centuries. Wallis was one of the founders of the Royal Society and a friend of Pepys for forty years. A man of wide reading and cultivation, his distinction as a mathematician was surpassed only by Isaac Newton (1642–1727), whom Pepys knew well enough to correspond respectfully with about the mathematical probabilities of dicing but with whom he was never intimate. Newton's imaginative and intellectual power was of a different order from Pepys's (and of anybody else's, come to that). But Wallis, who was Savilian Professor of Geometry at Oxford from 1649 to 1703 – an extraordinary tenure – was very much a man of Pepys's world.

Wallis's career was founded on his abilities as a cryptographer. He acted as a kind of one-man Bletchley Park, first for the Parliament in the Civil War, then for Oliver Cromwell, and finally for the restored monarchy. Indeed, his services were, after 1688, put at the disposal of William III. To survive as a trusted servant of so many and such different regimes called for tact and judgement as well as professional skill. Wallis always refused to divulge his methods and, a naturally humane man, could always leave passages undecoded if they were likely to cause avoidable trouble.

DR JOHN WALLIS
Sir Godfrey Kneller, 1701

Sir William Petty (1623–87)

❦

Another member of this remarkable group of brilliant and original minds with whom Pepys was on the friendliest terms was Sir William Petty. Petty, like Wallis, was largely self-educated but, like him, was appointed to a Professorship at Oxford (that of Anatomy), in 1651. Although he too was of a strongly mathematical turn of mind, applying or attempting to apply mathematics to such diverse subjects as social statistics, economics and even sense data such as taste or smell, he combined this speculative intelligence with a strongly practical and observant curiosity. The two sides of his nature were profitably engaged when, after serving as physician to Cromwell's army in Ireland, he was commissioned to make a survey of the conquered country, in order to divide the estates of the losers between the army and others who claimed a share in the loot. The speed and accuracy with which he did this won universal admiration, but he did not neglect the opportunity of making a handsome fortune for himself. Back in England at the Restoration he devoted a good deal of time and ingenuity to the design of a ship with a double-keel. Both Charles II and Pepys were much impressed and several experimental vessels were built, though ultimately without success. Much more productively, Petty joined with his friend Major Graunt in the first serious attempt at a scientific and mathematical study of social statistics, *Some Observations on the Bills of Mortality*. 'Political Arithmetic' as Petty called it had taken root.

Everybody – Charles II, Pepys, Evelyn, John Aubrey – agreed that Petty was marvellous company. 'He can be an excellent Droll (if he haz a mind to it) and will preach *extempore* incomparably, either the Presbyterian way, Independent, Cappucin frier or Jesuite.'

No doubt it was only his earlier death that prevented his portrait appearing in the knot of close friends that Pepys grouped round himself on the page from his print collection (reproduced on page 44).

SIR WILLIAM PETTY, Isaac Fuller, *c.*1640–51

Thomas Ken, F. Scheffer, c.1700

Thomas Ken (1637–1711)

The *Diary* tells us a great deal about the common life of the members of the Navy Board, living cheek by jowl in the handsome, well-appointed houses that went with the job. Another perquisite was the Navy Office pew in the parish church of St Olave's, Hart Street, where the bust of Elizabeth was so placed that her bereaved husband could see it at his weekly devotions. For a man of so pronounced an anti-clerical turn of mind and a far from other-worldly disposition, Pepys was an indefatigable sermon-taster. One of the clergymen whom he respected both as an intellect and as a man was Thomas Ken, whom he got to know very well when they were both sent out in 1683 to assist Lord Dartmouth in the evacuation of the short-lived colony of Tangier.

Ken was a Fellow of Winchester, publishing in 1674 his *Manual of Prayers for Winchester Scholars* to which he subsequently added the famous Morning and Evening hymns, 'Awake, my Soul' and 'Glory to thee, my God, this night', which are still sung. As a Canon of Winchester he refused the hospitality of his house to the King's mistress, Nell Gwyn, when the Court was paying a visit. Charles II, whose choice of bishops was commended by Dr Johnson, ordered that the next vacancy on the bench should go 'to the little black fellow that refused his lodging to poor Nelly'. Ken had previously dared to reprove William, Prince of Orange, the future William III, for his unkind treatment of his wife. William, though angry, admired his courage and, after 1688, did what he could to induce Ken (who was one of the seven bishops who had stood out against James II's Romanizing policy) to remain in his see. But Ken, like Pepys, felt unable to take the oaths, having sworn fealty to James II.

SIR GODFREY KNELLER (1646–1723)
AND SIR PETER LELY (1618–80)

SIR GODFREY KNELLER, Self-portrait, 1685

The men whose portraits are to be found in the print from Pepys's own collection were all of them either (where they were not both) professional colleagues or men of congruent tastes and interests with whom Pepys was in regular contact. This circle was enriched by tangential figures, such as Lord Somers (1651–1716), the Whig Lord Chancellor

Sir Peter Lely, Self-portrait, *c.*1660

who was also President of the Royal Society, a connoisseur and man of learning, but also with much closer contacts, such as that with Sir Godfrey Kneller from whom Pepys commissioned portraits of himself, of John Evelyn, of Dr Wallis and of James II. The King was sitting to the painter for this very picture when he heard that William of Orange had landed at Torbay.

Kneller's productivity was enormous and his temper easy. His greater predecessor as the favourite of Court and of high society, Sir Peter Lely, was, in Pepys's opinion 'mighty proud and full of state', a judgement that seems consonant with the self-portraits here reproduced. At the same time Pepys had no reservations about his pictures 'without doubt much beyond Mr Hales's' (whom he had commissioned to paint the famous portrait of himself (page 4) and that of his wife, destroyed, it is said, by an infuriated or inebriated cook, in the next century). Pepys also considered Lely far superior – 'Lord, the difference there is between their two works' – to John Michael Wright (1625?–1700), a portraitist much favoured by Cromwell's family and court as well as by that of Charles II. Pepys particularly admired Lely's portrait of Sandwich, his cousin and patron, 'very well done, and am with child till I get it copyed out' – a request that was soon granted: the copy, made by Emmanuel de Critz (1608–65), now hangs at Audley End.

HENRY PURCELL (1659–95)

❧

Music, of all the arts, was easily Pepys's favourite. It permeated his domestic and family life – social evenings were incomplete without instrumental music and even solitude could be enriched by singing (Pepys was a bass who could take that part in the choral services of the Chapel Royal). The greatest musician of his day, Henry Purcell was not, so far as we know, a friend or even an acquaintance of Pepys. But Pepys certainly knew of him, since both Purcell's father and uncle were musicians in the service of the court or the Chapel Royal. Some of his compositions are to be found in the musical collection that Pepys took such trouble to preserve and transcribe for his library – it was another interest that he shared with his cousin, Sandwich, whose own journal as ambassador in Madrid is full of details and drawings of Spanish musical instruments as well as of accounts of his own enjoyment of playing the guitar. 'Musick,' wrote Pepys reflectively in old age, 'a science peculiarly productive of a pleasure that no state of life, publick or private, secular or sacred: no difference of age or season; no temper of man's or condition of health exempt from present anguish; nor, lastly, distinction of quality, renders either improper, untimely or unentertaining.'

HENRY PURCELL, by or after John Closterman, 1695

THOMAS KILLIGREW, after Sir Anthony van Dyck, 17th century

Thomas Killigrew (1612–83)

When it came to entertainment it was to the theatre that Pepys, especially the young Pepys, eagerly hurried. Besides the dramatic or comic spell it cast on an audience starved of such excitements (the Puritans had closed the theatres for the twenty years that had preceded the Restoration) there was, once again, the pleasure of music and the allure of beautiful actresses. It was from the stage that Charles II had chosen two of his principal mistresses Moll Davis (*fl.*1663–9) and Nell Gwyn (1650–87), 'pretty, witty Nell' as Pepys called her. He did not himself fly so high in his amours but some of the ladies who gave Elizabeth Pepys grounds for doubting her husband's fidelity were connected with the stage.

Moll Davis, R. Thompson after Sir Peter Lely, *c.*1670

NELL GWYN, studio of Sir Peter Lely, c.1675

The one most frequently mentioned in the *Diary*, Elizabeth Knepp, was a member of the company put together by Thomas Killigrew, known as the King's Company, the rivals of the only other licensed body, the Duke's Company, run by Sir William Davenant. Killigrew, born into an aristocratic Cornish family, had begun to write plays before the Civil War. As a page to Charles I he was an avowed Royalist and followed Charles II into exile, acting for a time as his representative in Venice. But his disreputable conduct led to his expulsion from the Republic. He continued to write plays, some of them obscene, and enjoyed the King's favour as a witty companion who was allowed all the licence of a court jester. In 1663 he built the Theatre Royal, burned down a few years later, on the site of the present Drury Lane Theatre, in which he delighted Pepys and other theatre-goers by the innovation of movable scenery. In his conversations with Pepys, who found him 'a merry droll', he emphasised the importance of music and singing in theatrical presentations (particularly praising the talents of Mrs Knepp) and talked of producing an Italian opera, which seems to have come to nothing. He and his family exemplify the drunken, dissolute side of Restoration society of which Pepys's closest friends, such as Coventry, Evelyn and Houblon severely disapproved, but which the King himself freely countenanced.

Enough has been said to justify the claim that Pepys's circle was as wide as that of any man of his time. To have corresponded with Newton, to have gossiped and cracked jokes with the hangers-on of Charles II's court, to have listened, rapt, to the music of Purcell, Blow and Matthew Locke, to have frequented the studios of Lely and Kneller, to have sat in council with Clarendon and Shaftesbury, to have managed the conduct of naval warfare with Monck and Prince Rupert, to have watched Charles II and James II at close quarters in times of grave crisis that threatened the stability of the throne, to have – but, easy as it would be to extend this catalogue, enough is enough. The range of Pepys's pleasures as of his business, of his intellectual and aesthetic concerns, encompasses his age.

LIST OF ILLUSTRATIONS

CHARACTER SKETCHES
Other titles in the series

Elizabethan Writers
Charles Nicholl

The Romantic Poets and Their Circle
Richard Holmes

First World War Poets
Alan Judd and David Crane

The Bloomsbury Group
Frances Spalding

Dr Johnson, His Club and Other Friends
Jenny Uglow

The Pre-Raphaelites
Jan Marsh

The Irish Literary Movement
A. Norman Jeffares

Soho in the Fifties and Sixties
Jonathan Fryer

Tennyson and His Circle
Lynne Truss

Fitzrovia: London's Bohemia
Michael Bakewell

*Winner of the 1998 Gulbenkian Award for
Best Museum Publication*